PETITION

To: Kerryanne
Be blessed
and May you prosper
as your soul prosper

To: Kerry anne

Be blessed

and May your prosper

as your soul prosper

PETITION

The Keys That Open the Door to the Kingdom

Dr. Linda Molli Moriah

Foreword by R. Pepe Ramnath, PHD

Petition

Published by Tate Publishing & Enterprises, LLC
127 E. Trade Center Terrace | Mustang, Oklahoma 73064 USA
1.888.361.9473 | www.tatepublishing.com

Tate Publishing is committed to excellence in the publishing industry. The company reflects the philosophy established by the founders, based on Psalm 68:11,
"The Lord gave the word and great was the company of those who published it."

Cover design by Bill Francis Peralta
Interior design by Jomar Ouano

Published in the United States of America

ISBN: 978-1-68333-806-2
1. Religion / Christian Life / Prayer
2. Religion / Christian Life / Spiritual Growth
16.02.03

To my mom, whom I love dearly. She is the one who have taught me to be resilient and the value of hard work. I watched her firsthand working multiple jobs as a single mother raising the eleven of us. She taught me to pray and work and not to expect God himself to come down to feed me (those were her words). I thank you, Mom. It is because of you I am me!

> And God blessed them, and God said unto them, "Be fruitful, and multiply, and replenish the earth, and subdue it: and have dominion over the fish of the sea, and over the fowl of the air, and over every living thing that moveth upon the earth." (Gen. 1:28)

ACKNOWLEDGMENT

To my Father God, who gave me authority before the foundation of the world and restored me when I lost it, through the blood of Jesus Christ. To my sister in the kingdom, Linda Josephine White, who is always there to help me when I needed her assistance. To my spiritual father, Dr. Pepe Ramnath, and Pastor Angela Ramnath, who gave me a platform to stand on. Last but not least, my dear husband and children, who are my heroes. You all are my biggest cheerleaders. I am forever grateful to all of you.

FOREWORD

By R. Pepe Ramnath, PhD

If you have been looking for a deeper and a more exciting walk with God, you have picked up the right book. Dr Linda Moriah-Molli has unlocked the treasures of heaven as this book gives us practical illustrations of how to conquer the hopelessness and despairs of our present world situations. Many of us are taking experimental journeys into life without a proper communication with our creator through prayer.

We often find ourselves lost in the jungles of uncertainties and disillusionment that frustrate our existence. Living a life of routine mundane predictability can have us sometimes going around in circles, draining our energies and making life boring. This power tool that Dr. Linda has created contains instructions, experiences, and protocol that will point us into the direction of our destination. Sometimes all we have to do is stop and ask for direction. You can influence your environment and control your circumstances again by gleaning from the pages of this outstanding work. Allow the information on the pages of this thesaurus of wisdom to shine on the pathway of your destiny.

Let us stop today from tired living with unanswered prayers and go through all sixty-seven word of truths with the prayer already prescribed for you and allow heaven to speak to us through the pen of Dr. Linda Let the petals of each page in this book change our lives to purposeful living as we approach the throne of God for effective kingdom living on earth. Thank you, Linda for listening to the voice of God and releasing his instruction for us on earth. His kingdom come, and his will be done on earth through kingdom protocols and prayer. Again, thank you, Dr Linda Moriah-Molli, for taking the time to research and enrich our lives with your book on prayer.

—R. Pepe Ramnath, PhD
Research Scientist / UN-EO Ambassador Vienna-Austria
Author/Pastor, Miramar Kingdom
Community Center (MKCC)
Miramar, Florida

INTRODUCTION

Just like many others, I used to wonder why my prayers and petitions to God were never effective. I would plea and beg, but there were no changes in my situations. I was discouraged, just like many of you, and stopped going to prayer meetings. The word *petitions* means "to make or present a formal request to an authority, with respect to a particular cause" (Oxford dictionary). I did not understand the purpose of making such petition, the responsibility to obey, and the power that comes with it until I read the *Keys to the Kingdom* by Dr. Myles Munroe. God created laws that all of us, including Him, has to abide by. God will not violate His own word, and through all the Bible, God has used many to do what needed to be done. God even borrowed Mary's womb to come on earth and reclaim us back. Satan knew that God could not come right that moment to help Eve in the garden, but he promised to use the same woman to crush Satan's head. This was the very reasons He came and did what He promised.

As you know, God is a spirit, and spirit needs a body to function. He needs you and I to make petition to Him in order for Him to act. Petitions are the keys to the door (the blood of Jesus Christ). Jesus spent hours in prayer, and it took Him a moment to heal someone. You and I are spirit and body and are the only ones who are legally allowed to be on earth. Any spirit that does not have a body is here illegally. He gave us dominion and authority to be here. If you are sick and tired of your situation, discouraged, and don't see any way out, just like I was, and want to see change, understand that He said in Matthew 16:19, "And I will give unto thee the keys of the kingdom of heaven: and whatsoever thou shalt bind on earth shall be bound in heaven: and whatsoever thou shalt loose on earth shall be loosed in heaven." Use these keys to open the door to the plan and purpose He has for you to live in abundance of peace, health, and prosperity on earth. As ambassadors of His kingdom, it is an embarrassment to the King we represent to look sick and broke all the time. It will be for His good name for us to be healthy and prosper! He gets all the glory.

WORD OF TRUTH 1

I will tell my story as an overcomer, not for pity but as a testimony to help others to overcome. I am liberated, redeemed, set free, set apart by the blood. All cultural stigmas, generational curses are broken. The chain is broken—in Christ Jesus! (1 John 4:4, KJV).

Prayer 1

Dear Father in Heaven, I have heard that You are never late, seldom early, but always on time. When I think back through the experiences of my life, I can see the truth in that statement. Thank You for always being on time. Thank You for the lessons You have taught me through waiting, through suffering, through the storms and valleys, and for Your faithfulness always. Thank You for the rays of sun that peaked through the clouds in the way of rays of sunshine. Thank You for the sun that shone brightly after the storms and cloudy days, and for Your son who is my sun and shield, the Lord Jesus Christ. If You had always been on my time schedule, I wouldn't have learned much in life, so I am thankful that You are always on time according to Your schedule. I praise You for who You are and all You've done (Eccles. 3:11, KJV). May I be found worthy in Your sight through the blood of Jesus Christ. In His name I pray, amen.

Word of Truth 2

God is the King, Jesus is the Secretary of State, and the Holy Spirit is the CIA. We are the ambassadors! Our job is to bring people to the embassy to get a visa to the country of heaven! (2 Cor. 5:20, KJV).

Prayer 2

Dear Father, I know in my heart that Jesus is the Word of Life who gives eternal life (Ps. 119:11, KJV). I want to read and hear His Words, to remember them and hide them in my heart, to ingrain them into my life. I will love the Word of Life and cherish its message. Please give me boldness to share the Word of Life with those who don't know You. In Jesus's name I pray, amen.

Word of Truth 3

Your deeds will follow you. If you don't want to see a deed again, don't do it (Rev. 14:13, KJV).

Prayer 3

Dear Dad in Heaven, may Your desires become my own desires. May I learn to "present my body as a living sacrifice to You" (Rom. 12:1, KJV). For I want to do what is right and pleasing to You. I want to obey, which Your Word says is even better than sacrifice. In this world, "there is a way that seems right to a man," but man's way is often not the right way and leads to sin and death. I understand there is a right way to talk, dress, act, look, live. Though I am in this world, I am not to be part of this world. Your Word tells me to "be holy because I am holy." Through the power of Your Holy Spirit, I can—and by Your grace, I will. Thank You for working to transform me by the renewing of my mind into the person You would have me be for Your glory. In Jesus's name I pray, amen.

WORD OF TRUTH 4

You cannot appreciate and honor something you have not acknowledged (Matt. 15:8, KJV).

Prayer 4

Dear Father, thank You for all of the special people You have placed in my life to complete me. Thank You for my few friends who are truly friends, for my soul mate, for my kingdom brothers and sisters. I pray now for those who do not have a special person to complete their lives. Please send the right person along who can be the one to offer encouragement, friendship, loving guidance, unconditional love, and to just be there. I pray that a bond of Christ's love will develop and that people will be uplifted. Please forgive me for not always letting my special people know how much they mean and help me to show them their importance in my life. I praise You and thank You for always being there for me too and for Your promise to never leave nor forsake me (Deut. 33:6, KJV). In Jesus's name I pray, amen.

Word of Truth 5

Religion tells you that you are a servant of the Lord, but the kingdom makes you sons and daughters of God (2 Cor. 6:18, KJV).

Prayer 5

Oh, dear Father, thank You for opening Your arms and welcoming me to come to You, to find rest in You, to find freedom in You, to have abundant life in You (John 10:10, KJV). I cry out to You now for those who are heavy on my heart, for those who are going through the fire and those who are going through the valleys, for those who face difficulties and those who have come through trials and are triumphant because of You. I pray for Your grace and mercy, Your peace and love, Your hand upon their lives. I pray for miracles and ministries. I pray that all who are weary will cry out to You and trust You. And I thank You so much for all that You have done and all that You will do. May Your works and miracles in our lives be witness to the world that You are God. May You be glorified and souls are saved. In the name of Jesus I pray, amen.

Word of Truth 6

> What you will receive will always be better and bigger than what you trying to hold on to. An open hand receives more than a closed fist! (Prov. 18:16, KJV).

Prayer 6

God, You are working, and all Your angels' army are battling on my behalf. My God is up to something, a new day to start anew, and we exalt Thee, Lord, and may we be glad this day. Pour Your blessings upon us for we need You to get through this day. Lord, the poor, the sick and the widows need You now. There are so many people without hope of a better tomorrow. Lord let Your Holy Spirit touch them and move them to call to You. We are all created for Your glory, and let us gaze upon that glory. Let Your kingdom come on earth and awaken Your Spirit within us to make us all realize we are all kings and queens in Your kingdom. Lift our burden, and make today be a day of victory in You. In Jesus Your son's name, amen.

Word of Truth 7

The Holy Spirit will search you and will be your greatest Psychologist ever. He will arrest you if He has to and make you listen! Your heart will be open when He touched you. So be careful all fake pastors, fake ministers and fake prophets. You will be judged! Selah! (1 Cor. 2:10, KJV).

Prayer 7

Dear God, I want to recommit myself to You, to do Your good will, to follow Your word and the guidance of Your Holy Spirit. I want to draw closer to You in word, thought, and deed. I want to have an attitude of gratitude, a smile on my face and in my voice, and energy to do whatever task or ministry You want me to do. Please continue to provide my every need, as only You can do. Please bless me that I may be a blessing to others. Please give me wisdom, knowledge, desire, and power to go forth and live for You to make a difference in the lives of those around me and to glorify You. Please bless my coming and my going, and open my mouth to speak words of truth and love (Ps. 121:8, KJV). Thank You, God. In Jesus's name I pray, amen.

Word of Truth 8

The true reason Jesus came is for you to be free. The message doesn't suppress and enslave people. It is meant to liberate you (Gal. 5:1, KJV).

Prayer 8

Good day, Father! Thank You for this day. Thank You for times when I can step back and reflect. (Ps. 46:1, KJV). I realize that through the years, I have developed habits that are irritating to You and to my family too. Please help me to change that. I only want to have good habits. I pray that I will be a blessing to You, to my family, to my friends, and everyone I meet. Please forgive me of my sins and failures, of the times I have not been kind to my family, of those annoying little habits. I commit to You today that with Your help, I will change for the better. I praise and worship You, Lord. In Jesus's name, amen!

Word of Truth 9

As you pray each morning, God is reading the book on your life so you can do his will for your life. Not just pray but allow him to teach you how to do his will so you do not harbor iniquity in your heart. He will take you through the storm, strengthen you, and make you leap over walls. He is the King of kings, and his will prevails! (Ps. 139:16, KJV).

Prayer 9

Oh God, time and grace heals our wounds, but time is not always a *friend*. What about my friends who have not heard Your words of life? What if they were to die today? I should know how short life can be. I've lost loved ones and friends who were young. Accidents and sudden illness can take away a life quickly. Cancer, diabetes, aneurysms, catastrophic events can change a person's health and life in a moment. Lord, why do I fear opening my mouth? Please help me to be bold then speak Your words of truth and life to those I love, my family and friends, before time runs out. Help me to be a living testimony for You. Stir up the Holy Spirit within me and the gifts You have given me to minister to others, to reach a dying world, to share Your love and Your hope for the future (Col. 1:27, KJV).Thank You in the name of Jesus, my Lord and Savior. Amen.

WORD OF TRUTH 10

God's eye is on the rejected, and He is raising them up as leaders! Don't ignore the third world people. It's time things change! (Matt. 21:42, KJV).

Prayers 10

Dear Father God, truly blessed is the feet of those who share the good news of the gospel of Jesus Christ, a gospel of the kingdom (Matt. 24:14). I pray for every Christian and every Christian leader who shares Your love and gift of life with others. I pray for protection and blessing upon those lives. I pray that You will give each of us the messages that You want us to speak and nudge us through Your Holy Spirit to speak at the right times and the right places. Through Your power, may the world know that You are God, and through our ministries may You be glorified, souls saved, and Christians united in strength and love. In the Savior's name I pray, amen.

Word of Truth 11

Whatever you give will reciprocate back to you. You want love, give love. You want respect, give respect. Honor others, and you will not be dishonored (Luke 6:38, KJV).

Prayer 11

Dear Lord, I rejoice that You make all things new! You can even raise a dead marriage to new life. I choose to look ahead, not behind, in my marriage. I choose not to call to mind hurts from the past. I can't wait to see what good things You bring to my marriage as I trust and obey You. In Jesus's name, amen.

Word of Truth 12

The devil convinces the world he didn't exist, so many are being deceived! (2 Cor. 11:3, KJV).

Prayer 12

Happy day, Father! (Josh. 1:9, KJV). I pray for all the fathers in the world, that You would encourage them today, draw them to You, and give them wisdom for the responsibilities they have as fathers. Please bless all the wonderful fathers, convict and instruct those who have failed as fathers, and help us all to remember how special fathers are. I thank You for my father and for all the fathers who are in heaven and are being missed today. Please comfort the children, young and old, who have an absent father, whether through death, military duty, desertion, job travels, or whatever reason. Thank You, God, for families and the love most families share. In Jesus's name, amen.

Word of Truth 13

Do you know when one kingdom citizen wakes up, the devil goes, "Oh my, I am in trouble." When we rise up and glorify God the Father, the Son, and the Holy Spirit, he flees. So rise up, army of God. Give Him glory for He is the King (James 4:7, KJV).

Prayer 13

I pray that You will raise Your standard on the earth, Lord, and let Your people rise up to proclaim Your name (Isa. 59:19, KJV). Let Your light shine through the darkest heart and soften it. Touch the heart of those who are depressed during this time, and lift up the cloud from their mind. Send someone who brings rays of sunshine in their lives. Lord, strengthen the ones who are sick, and restore their bodies. I pray for families that are broken apart, that You will heal their hearts. I thank You, Adonai, holy one. You reign. I thank You in the name of Your son Jesus. Amen and Amen.

Word of Truth 14

The story of Ruth is how grace happens in hard times. Let me spell it out! Jesus is your kinsman-redeemer. He spotted you in the wheat field, ramshackled by hurt. And He has resolved to romance your heart through sunsets, whispers of scripture. Are you marginalized and discarded? Others may think so. You may think so. But God sees in you a masterpiece about to happen. Grace! God walking into your life with sparkles in His eye. (Gal. 4:4–7, KJV).

Prayer 14

Oh dear Lord, thank You for Your promises! (Jer. 29:11, KJV). Thank You for opening Your arms and welcoming me to come to You, to find rest in You, to find freedom in You, to have abundant life in You. I cry out to You now for those who are heavy on my heart, for those who are going through the fire and those who are going through the valleys, for those who face difficulties and those who have come through trials and are triumphant because of You. I pray for Your grace and mercy, Your peace and love, Your hand upon their lives. I pray for miracles and ministries. I pray that all who are weary will cry out to You and trust You. And I thank You so much for all that You have done and all that You will do. May Your works and miracles in our lives be witness to the world that You are God! May You be glorified and souls are saved. In the name of Jesus I pray, amen.

Word of Truth 15

God does not dwell in temple made by men but in your body that is created by him. You are the temple of the Holy Spirit (1 Cor. 6:19, KJV).

Prayer 15

I war in the name of Jesus—by the shed blood of Jesus Christ! Deliver me from emotional blackmail. Free me from limitations! I break through glass ceilings! I wear a cloak of favor. His miracle is manifested in my life—for his glory! In Jesus's name, amen!

Word of Truth 16

Never eat your seed. A nation starved because they ate their seed. You have to cultivate your seed and plant it to pick the fruit (Prov. 11:24, KJV).

Prayer 16

My Father in heaven, thank *You* that for every hurt, every fear, every worry, every need, there is a remedy—through the power of the resurrection, the presence of the Holy Spirit, and the care of the Almighty, everything is going to be all right. As long as You are in control of my life, everything is going to be all right. I cling to the Savior's invitation to "come unto me, all ye that labor and are heavy laden, and I will give you rest. Take my yoke upon you, and learn of me; for I am meek and lowly in heart: and ye shall find rest to your souls. For my yoke is easy, and my burden is light" (Matt. 11:28–30, KJV). I praise You, Father, for loving me so much that You sent Your only begotten son, full of grace and truth, to take my sins upon Him that I might be made righteous in our sight. Thank You for the tremendous sacrifice, for our love and mercy, for life eternal, for being all that really matters—for being my Remedy. I love You. In the name of Jesus, amen.

Word of Truth 17

I don't want a piece of the pie. I want the whole *enchilada*! I remove the mask that defines me. Unashamed, liberated, not afraid, confident and no masquerade! *I am that woman!*

(Eph. 3:20, KJV).

Prayer 17

Dear Jehovah Jireh, You are the Lord, my provider. You provide hope for hopeless, love for the unlovely, life for the dead in sin, wisdom for those who ask for it, a way out for those who are tempted, the way forward for those who seek You, a hand up for those who have fallen, the Light to bring people out of the darkness, the Bread of Life and Water of Life for those who are spiritually hungry and thirsty, peace within for those who trust in You—and so much more (John 6:35, KJV). Can I even count the ways You provide? I acknowledge Your loving provision for my needs, oh Mighty God, Jehovah Jireh. You truly are the Provider. Thank You from the depths of my heart. In the name of Jesus I pray, amen.

WORD OF TRUTH 18

Whenever you are separated from your source, your spirit man is dead. Think of when you don't charge your phone, it dies (Rom. 6:23, KJV).

Prayer 18

My Heavenly Father, calm my spirit today. Please forgive me of gossip or worry about the people and circumstances that surround me. Please replace anger with peace. Please help me to keep my focus on Jesus, author and finisher of my faith (Heb. 12:2, KJV). Please help me to focus on what I need to accomplish today and what You want me to do. Put away all wrong thoughts, and keep me from wrong actions. I want to be a steady, stable, godly person who is a pleasure to be around and a loving witness of Your mercy and glory. May I be an instrument that produces a sweet, soothing sound, uplifting spirits and pleasing the Master Conductor, My Lord. In Jesus's name I pray, amen.

Word of Truth 19

We do not serve a God that is speechless. So listen. Otherwise, you will make unwise decision

(Jer. 33:3, KJV).

Prayer 19

Dear Father God, I know You want me to have a complete picture of the situations I face each day and to know what actions I must take to fulfill Your will for my life. I thank You for the Holy Spirit who prays on my behalf when I just don't have the words to day. Thank You for Jesus, who is the great Intercessor who stands in the gap and intercedes for me. Please bring intercessors and leaders into my life to hold me up in prayer and help me along the way (Rom. 8:34, KJV). Likewise, help me be an intercessory prayer warrior, praying and interceding on the behalf of others around me who need prayer for special needs and daily struggles. Bless me, Father, and enlarge my territory. Be with me and keep me from evil that I may be a blessing to You and to those around me. In the name of my Lord and Savior I pray, amen.

WORD OF TRUTH 20

If you only believe, you will see the glory of God manifest in your life today in the form of miracles! (Matt. 21:22, KJV).

Prayer 20

Dear Father God, I am acutely aware of those who are sick and suffering today. I lift up the babies who have been born with deformities or medical problems that require intervention and need Your healing touch. May Your grace and Your loving touch envelop them and their families. I pray for those who have viruses, illnesses, or allergies that affect so many. I pray for relief of pain and symptoms—and for Your healing touch. I pray for those who are battling other more serious medical issues, whether heart problems, cancer, and even blood clots or diabetes that can lead to disastrous consequences. Please guide the doctors who treat these people that they will know what to do. Please help each and every afflicted one to know what to do to improve their situation—if anything. You are our Healer (Exod. 15:26). Please provide Your comfort, and cover each one in need with Your warmth, Your presence, and Your miraculous healing power. Thank You, Lord, for hearing my prayer. In Jesus's name, amen.

Word of Truth 21

When God likes you, nobody else matters! (Rom. 9:25, KJV).

Prayer 21

Lord, You are the Potter; I am the clay (Isa. 64:8, KJV). Please mold me and make me, according to Your will. Show me the steps, and direct my ways that all I do will be Your will for my life, that Your purpose may be accomplished. To You be all glory and honor. In Jesus's name, amen.

WORD OF TRUTH 22

The God who answers by fire will answer you today. He will trouble who troubles you (Exod. 14:14, KJV).

Prayer 22

Dear Father God, I thank You this morning for the Rock of my salvation. I thank You that my life can be built upon a strong foundation. Please help me to trust, to live, to take every breath based upon the foundation I have in You. Please help me to weather life's storms, to keep looking to You, and to be a thankful child—never a pouting brat. I pray that you will strengthen me and keep my feet steady on solid ground (Ps. 121:3, KJV). I pray for my family members, Lord, that each one will be committed to You and live a life that glorifies You and ministers to others. In the blessed name of Jesus I pray, amen.

Word of Truth 23

If you don't know what you're aiming for, you will hit your target every time (Prov. 16:3, KJV).

Prayer 23

Lord, You are the vine, and I am a branch. I want to abide in You and You in me so that I will bear much fruit, for without You I can do nothing. If I abide in You and Your words abide in me, I will ask what I desire, and it shall be done for me. I pray that Your desires will be my desires; that Your Word will be held close in my heart. By this our Father is glorified, that I bear much fruit, so I will be Your disciple. Thank You for loving me and accepting me as Your child and disciple. I pray that I will always remain full of Your joy and love others as You have loved me (John 15:5–12, KJV). In Your name I pray, amen.

Word of Truth 24

Everything will be left unfulfilled if you fail as a family (Deut. 5:9, KJV).

Prayer 24

Dear God, thank You for having a purpose for my life and for telling me what Your expectations are through the Bible. I know You must be disappointed with me many times when I fail to meet Your expectations of me. I can identify with that from a human standpoint. When I expect a family member to be responsible and to do something that they do not do, or when they make wrong choices in life, I am very disappointed. Sometimes I feel frustrated or angry and other times heartbroken. Help me to be kindhearted and long-suffering with them like You are with me. Guide me to handle those disappointments with integrity, to remain quiet when I should, and to speak up when I should. Please give me the thoughts, words, and actions You want me to have. And God, please forgive me for disappointing You. In Jesus's name I pray, amen.

WORD OF TRUTH 25

Excuses is a tool of incompetence that build a bridge to nowhere. (Col. 3:23, KJV).

Prayer 25

Dear Father God, why does the human mind doubt and worry? I know in my heart that no matter what, You have "got my back." I trust that all things will work to the good of those who love You (Rom. 8:28, KJV). I believe in my Savior Jesus and Your promises of hope and a future. Come what may, You are here with me and will never forsake me. Please calm my worries, cast out all doubt, and reassure me through the peace of Your Spirit. Thank You for always providing in Your perfect timing. You are truly amazing. Thank You for Your Strong Consolation—Jesus Christ—in whose name I pray. Amen.

Word of Truth 26

You can't give what you don't have! I am telling you to pray for wisdom! (2 Cor. 8:12, KJV).

Prayer 26

Today is a brand new day to begin again! Make it a great one! Yesterday memories may not be so good. Make new memories today! Command your day because day speaks! (Ps. 19:2, KJV). Let your day ask what he can do for you! Squeeze every second out of every single minute! Come out of bed swinging, giving thanks to the Almighty God! You are here now! Thank You, God Almighty, for life. We praise Your name and are grateful for the ones waking up this morning. May You enlightened the masses to bow before Your throne. In Jesus's mighty name, amen.

WORD OF TRUTH 27

The word of God is brutally honest!(2 Sam. 7:28, KJV).

Prayer 27

Dear Father, it is You who arms me with strength and makes my way perfect. Thank You for making my feet like the feet of a deer, enabling me to stand on the heights. Thank You for training my hands for daily obstacles, battles, and spiritual hurdles. Thank You for giving me Your shield of victory. Thank You for broadening the path beneath me so that my ankles do not turn (based on 2 Samuel 22:33–37, kjv). I praise and worship You, Almighty God. I trust You to work in me to keep my feet on solid ground and to help me be a witness of Your saving grace to my family, friends, coworkers, and neighbors. May all glory and honor be unto You. In Jesus's name, amen.

Word of Truth 28

Integrity is the prerequisite for lasting change (Prov. 10:9, KJV).

Prayer 28

I woke up with thanksgiving in my lips and gratitude in my heart. I command my morning that today will bring me joy and make the labor of my hand bear fruit! I command the day to show me the unfailing love of my father and shake evil out of my sphere of influence. No evil shall come near my tent. The anointing of the Lord that comes upon me shall make all laws, ordinances, and regulations work in my favor according to God's plan for me. I command everything to align with the plan of God. Any plan of the enemy that is set to attack my marriage, my loved ones, my family, I command that you get out right now, backed by Jesus's name! Anything that affects me negatively, move out of the way! I degree and declare health, prosperity, sound mind. I wear a cloak of favor. I am a child of God. I am redeemed by the blood of the lamb. Therefore, no evil shall befall me. I shall live and not die. I am a kinsman of Jesus. May this prayer rise up. In Jesus's name, amen!

Word of Truth 29

Where there is great love, there will always be great sacrifices (1 John 4:10, KJV).

Prayer 29

Dear God, I'm thirsty. I'm thirsty for Your anointing on my life and ministry, for Your Living Water of life. Please increase my hunger for Your Word and Your will, keep my heart humble, and strengthen my commitment to Your ways. I need my heart's desire to be for You. I want more of You, God. Please forgive my frailties and strengthen my spirit. Help me to feel Your presence and experience Your power as never before. Shine through me to touch the lost and dying world around me for their good and Your glory. Please shower me with Your blessings that I may soak up those blessings, share them with others, and be a blessing to You. In Your name I pray, amen.

Word of Truth 30

Great prayers champion God's agenda! (Prov. 19:21, KJV).

Prayer 30

"He who dwells in the shelter of the Most High will abide in the shadow of the Almighty" (Ps. 91:1, ESV). Dear God, though manmade shelter may fall in the storms and fury of nature and war, nothing can destroy the strong and everlasting shelter I have in the shadow of the all-powerful Almighty God. Thank You for keeping my soul and calming my spirit. I pray for those who are being affected by tornadoes, cyclones, and other storms of nature. Please protect them, provide their needs, and comfort those who have lost their shelter and possessions in storms that have passed through. May every need be met through Your grace, mercy, and the assistance of the church, volunteers, and government aid where appropriate. In the name of my precious Savior, Jesus, amen.

WORD OF TRUTH 31

Your values determine your evaluation. If you value material and physical things, trials will upset you. If you value the spiritual, you will appreciate trials and understand God's plan for you. Count it all joy! (James 1:2, KJV).

Prayer 31

Dear God, let me begin by thanking You for taking care of me and my family, for being there to carry us and protect us and love us for eternity. God, please inspire me from within, through Your Holy Spirit, with fresh ideas for showing Your love to my neighbors, friends, family, and all who are needy in some way. Please guide me and minister through me to do Your will each and every day. Let me be a blessing in Your name. Let my face radiate from the joy of my salvation and the peace of Your Spirit. Let my smile encourage others and my attitude be one of gratitude and hope. Let the words from my mouth speak praise, admonition, and truth in love. May the fruits of Your Holy Spirit grow within me and spill out of me, overflowing and abundant. I praise You this day for everything and want to always be grateful to You. In the name of Jesus Christ, Your precious son and my Lord and Savior, I pray, amen.

WORD OF TRUTH 32

Praise God all is well. Be aware of false prophets that preach end of the world (Matt. 7:15, KJV).

Prayer 32

Dear Lord, many are the wonderful works You have done. You have put a new song in my mouth and praise in my heart. You gave new life to my steps and peace in my soul. You have lifted me up and placed me upon solid ground. Thank you. May my life bless You and my words exalt You, O Lord. In Jesus's name, amen.

WORD OF TRUTH 33

Great prayers are deeply personal and birth out of brokenness! (Ps. 34:18, KJV).

Prayer 33

Dear Father, I thank You for the son and for giving me the chance to have a relationship with Him. He is the Vine, and I am the branch. I abide in Him and He abides in me. Without the Vine, the branch cannot exist. I thank You for giving me strength each day, and I ask that You help me to become what I am striving to be. I want to be more like Jesus, who is my kinsman-redeemer. I thank You for Your mercy and grace. In Jesus's mighty name I pray, amen!

Word of Truth 34

You need to convince and cheer yourself up that He who created you will turn your situations around for good. So do not be limited by what you see; see beyond and take steps to change (2 Cor. 4:18, KJV).

Prayer 34

Father God, I found out there is power in the name of Your son Jesus to break every chain in my life. So today I shout out His name and break every chain. I shout out until I hear the chain falling. Break away from everything that was holding me back. Break away from poverty. Break away from health issues, family bondage, and anything that was affecting me negatively. I declare that I am free today and dance my freedom dance. I am liberated, for my mind is no longer the same. I thank You for Your son, and in His name I pray, amen!

WORD OF TRUTH 35

My God is a God of possibilities! Do not miss out! (Matt. 19:26, KJV).

Prayer 35

Father God, today I came out to give You a shout-out! I pray that You remove all my limitations, the one that I put on myself and the ones that others are trying to put on me. I pray that You remove everything that is covering my spiritual eyes and blocking my vision. Please give me 20/20 vision in the spiritual. Give me a hearing so sharp that I don't miss anything Your Spirit is telling me. I am patiently waiting on You for this petition. In Jesus's name I pray, amen!

Word of Truth 36

You can't live in freedom if you keep doing the same thing that has kept you in bondage (Gal. 5:1, KJV).

Prayer 36

Father God, I believe to the core of my being that Your Son died and rose up on the third day. You promise to redeem me, and You did, and the shackle has broken. Please manifest Your Holy Spirit in me so I can continue to stay free and liberated. I thank You for Your Son, and I thank You for the anointing. You are a gracious God who is the only one that is able to cleanse me through the blood. I thank You, everlasting Father. In Jesus's name I pray, amen.

WORD OF TRUTH 37

There is much reward in righteous living! (Ps. 5:12, KJV).

Prayer 37

Dear Father in heaven, I come before You today in remembrance on how You set me free and that I am no longer bound by the enemy. I am free, and I have the power to be holy, power to live in Your Son Jesus. I am walking in freedom, and I am shouting that I am no longer in that prison. I pray that You bestow Your grace upon me to continue to see that and walk in that freedom. Pour Your grace to increase my belief in what You have already done. I need Your grace to walk in the area that I had struggle in, walking in confidence in what You have called me to be. I receive that grace. Almighty and all-powerful God, help me to be bold for You. In Jesus's name I pray, amen!

Word of Truth 38

To be motivated on the inside is better than motivated outwardly (1 Sam. 16:7, KJV).

Prayer 38

Father, You are God alone sitting on the throne, and You never change. Through the good times and my bad times, You stay the same. You are the only constant thing in my life. So I call on You through the storm and the smooth-sailing period of my live. Your promises are truth, and it will come to pass in my life. Age to age You have stood and have raised Your standard against the enemy that was trying to overtake me. You keep me steady no matter the circumstances. I thank You for Your grace and mercy, and to You belongs all the honor and glory! In Jesus's name I pray, amen.

Word of Truth 39

You can only accomplish as far as your thought can lead you! (Prov. 4:23, KJV).

Prayer 39

Dear Father, there is no one greater than You as I come humbly before Your throne. I am lifting my spirit, mind, and body to You. For You are the only one who can heal my broken heart. You are the great I AM. I look all over searching until I found You. There is no one who is stronger or wiser than You. You are bigger than any struggle I may have, any debt I owe, any doubt and insecure feelings. I pray that You continue to fill me with Your Spirit. Continue to strengthen me to do what You called me to be. I thank You, gracious God. In Jesus's name I pray, amen.

Word of Truth 40

There is no reaping without sowing is the law of harvest!
(2 Cor. 9:6, KJV).

Prayer 40

Dear Father, You are a God who is so big, and at times as a human, we reduce You to our own level just to comprehend who You are. You are a big God, and we are doing You injustice by reducing You to a human size. I ask that You forgive me if at times my mind did not understand Your greatness. I ask that You continue to open my mind and expand my intellectual territory and give me understanding and wisdom to see who You are. Let Your grace abound over and over again in my life as I am sure to continue walking with You. I thank You, Father, in Jesus's name. Amen!

Word of Truth 41

Close the gap between talking and doing for therein lies your freedom (James 1:23–25, KJV).

Prayer 41

Abba, Father, You are love. Your Word tells me that; experience shows me that. I remember singing the children's song "Praise Him, Praise Him, all ye little children. God is love, God is love…" Yes, You are worthy of our praise and honor. Whether I feel down and out, unloved; am going through trials and tough times; or when I'm happy, prosperous, and on top of the mountain, Your love reaches me. Your presence surrounds me and brings me warmth, contentment, and peace. Thank You, Father, so much for that. In Jesus's name I pray and give You praise, amen.

Word of Truth 42

Remember the difference between the creation and the Creator! (Rom. 1:25, KJV).

Prayer 42

Dear God, thank You for this day. Sometimes my world just seems dark, problems abound, stress creeps in; I can't seem to see the light at the end of the tunnel. But I know You are there to carry me through. Your Word tells me that "weeping may endure for a night, but joy comes in the morning" (Ps. 30:5, AMP), so I have hope and Your promise of joy. Please continue to lift me up, give me strength, and carry me when necessary so that I may emerge victorious over the darkness and continually be filled with joy and praise. Thank You. In Jesus's name, amen.

Word of Truth 43

Falling in love is not a good enough reason to get married. Commitment to one another is (1 Sam. 16:7, KJV).

Prayer 43

Oh, my Elohim-Selichot, God of Forgiveness. I am so grateful for Your grace and forgiveness. I am so blessed to be covered by the sacrifice of Jesus, lifted by the intercession of the Holy Spirit, and loved by You, my Heavenly Father. What more could I need? If I should lose my earthly life today, I would be worshipping with the angels, praising with the saints, and basking in the glow of Your presence in my heavenly home where there is no more sin, no more pain, no more worries, no more suffering—fully free at last. My Elohim-Selichot, God of Forgiveness, You are awesome, and I love You. In the blessed name of Jesus I pray, amen.

Word of Truth 44

People are teaching you things that they have not done themselves (Theory). (Proverbs 13:20, KJV).

Prayer 44

Dear Lord, thank You for this day. Thank You for my being able to see, to hear, to speak, to move about this morning. I'm blessed because You are a forgiving and understanding God. You have done so much for me. I have witnessed Your hand of blessing, Your miraculous power in my life and the lives of those I love, and You just keep on blessing me. Forgive me this day for everything I have done, said, or thought that was not pleasing to You. I ask now for Your forgiveness. Please keep me, my family, and my church family safe from all danger and harm. Help me to start this day with a positive and Christ-focused attitude and plenty of gratitude. Please clear my mind of distractions so that I can hear from You, and please direct my steps today. Thank You so much. In Jesus's name, amen.

Word of Truth 45

You can't be a Joshua man with a Moses blueprint. Thou shall not lead beyond your own exposure! Your level of exposure determines how far you can go (1 Kings 4:29, KJV).

Prayer 45

Dear God, thank You so much that you are there for me always; that if I stumble and fall, I will fall into Your grace. I praise You, my rescuer and one who loves me more than life. I bow before You in prayer, with a humble spirit and grateful heart. You are my stability in a world gone mad, my comfort when my heart is sad. You give me sunshine in every day. I pray this day that my loved ones are healthy, happy, and don't lack any good things. May Your kingdom rule in their lives. In Jesus's name I pray, amen!

WORD OF TRUTH 46

Sometimes we are surrounded by people that if we fall, they couldn't catch us (Eccles. 4:10, KJV).

Prayer 46

Dear God, we all make mistakes—all humans that is. We all pay consequences, often not easy to deal with. Some mistakes affect our health, our jobs, our rights, our futures, our comfort, and our ministries. They usually involve other people's lives, not just our own. All mistakes give opportunity for life-changing lessons. I pray for anyone and everyone who is spending time with you through this devotional and for their family members who have made mistakes and are facing the consequences. May the result be a life that is more dedicated to You, one that is pleasing to You, and clarity of purpose and calling in the lives that are affected! I pray for mercy, grace, and help in any way needed. May You be glorified! May new ministries and opportunities for witness be evident, and may each one of us be yielded and in tune with Your will. Please help us all to become what You have planned for us. Thank You, Father, for Your work in our lives and for Your protection and blessing. In the name of Jesus I pray, amen.

WORD OF TRUTH 47

God is raising you to touch the new generation! Not just for your own benefit! (Gen. 22:18, KJV).

Prayer 47

Dear Father God, I know that You want me to be like salt on the earth, like a candle in the dark, a lighthouse on a hill, so that others will come to You. Cleanse me anew that I will be a witness for You. Show me how You want to penetrate the darkness of my domain with Your light. Help me to be a positive influence in the places where I live, work, study, play. Thank You, Lord. In the name of Jesus, amen.

Word of Truth 48

Attacks don't come from the enemy but from the frenemy (Ps. 55:12–14, KJV).

Prayer 48

Jeremiah 29:11 says that Your plan for me is for good and not for evil, to give me a better future. Father, I pray that the enemy will not overtake me. Based on the book of Exodus, the enemy has been pursuing me since the day I was born. But Lord, You will not allow that because the blood of Jesus has stopped that. Any devise the enemy plans is destroyed, for I trust in You to fight my battle. In You I am more than a conqueror. You make my hand strong, and You will destroy the destroyer of my marriage, my finance, my family, and the blood of Jesus is fighting on my behalf. All this I ask shall be done by my Father in heaven! In Jesus's name I pray, amen!

Word of Truth 49

Failure is not God's ultimate plan for you, so don't give up. Lay it before Him, and be persistent and diligent. Then your hard work will be rewarded!

(Eph. 1:11, KJV).

Prayer 49

Father God, Your plan for me is to take me to higher highs and set my feet as the hind's feet. I take courage in Your son, who leads by example, and through him I am strong to stand. I pray that You continue to expand my understanding to do Your will. You said in Proverbs that a diligent hand will not beg for bread. I know that You will bring forth my helper to assist me in Your plan for my life. I thank You, faithful God, for You are my strength. I so pray in Jesus's mighty name, amen!

WORD OF TRUTH 50

You are wired with the desire to belong, so don't go where you're just tolerated (John 15:5, KJV).

Prayer 50

My precious Heavenly Father, here I am to worship You this day. Here I am to declare that You are my God and lift up Your name. I praise You above all on the earth and above every being in the heavens. You are the almighty, all-powerful, and all-knowing God that I come to. You hold me in Your hand and watch over me. Thank You for shielding me and loving me. Thank You for Your tender mercies and Your firm chastisement, oh One who loves more than any other loves. Thank You for reminding me of who You are and who I am. Without You, I am nothing. With You, I am forgiven, blessed, and victorious. Through the blood of Jesus, I am made righteous. I cannot thank You enough for saving my soul and carrying me through this life. In Jesus's name, I bow before You. Amen.

Word of Truth 51

Turbulent times let us forget that God sometimes stay on course no matter the storm. He will get you through this, and it won't be quick, but He will (Ps. 23:1–6, KJV).

Prayer 51

Dear God, I pray for all those who are reading this devotional e-mail that You will touch their lives in great and mighty ways. Please draw them closer to You and provide comfort on difficult days, smiles when sadness intrudes, rainbows to follow the clouds, laughter to kiss their lips, sunsets to warm their hearts, gentle hugs when spirits sag, friendships to brighten their being, beauty for their eyes to see, confidence for when they doubt, faith so that they can believe, courage to know themselves, patience to accept the truth, and love to complete their lives. Thank You, God, for Your blessings. In Jesus's name I pray, amen.

Word of Truth 52

God is good—he will not change—even if life isn't (Mal. 3:6, KJV).

Prayer 52

Dear awesome Father in heaven, I praise Your name, which is above all names. I lift up to You all those who are weary in their labors. I pray for strength, encouragement, peace, motivation, wisdom, guidance, rest, and for provision for their every need. Please have mercy and lift them up through the power and help that only You can give. I know that You will answer the cries of their hearts, that You will revive their exhausted minds and bodies, that You will invigorate their spirits if they will only trust in You to be their ever-present help. Help those who suffer from unbelief that they will believe as they see Your love and power at work in their lives. Bless those who love You, Father. Thank You. In the name of Jesus, who promised to give rest to those who are weary and heavy-laden, amen.

Word of Truth 53

Attitude of the world owes you will make life twice as hard. Gratitude will make life easy to live and give you a joyful heart. (Romans 1:21, KJV).

Prayer 53

Dear Lord, how amazing it is to compare our life to the caterpillar that is surrounded by the cocoon and struggles until it emerges as a beautiful butterfly. I pray that as I struggle through life's challenges, I lean on You and allow the cocoon of Your love to surround me and the circumstances and trials to help mold me into the beautiful creature You want me to become. Thank You for all You do. In Jesus's name, amen.

Word of Truth 54

Grace is the gift that covers all sins. Relax, it's paid! (Rom. 11:16, KJV).

Prayer 54

Father God, You are the Almighty who sent Jesus, who proved mighty in deed and word. You are mighty to save, mighty to heal, mighty to provide, mighty to redeem, mighty to love. Your might is strong and more than worthy of my faith and trust. Thank You for Your mighty arms that carry me, love me, discipline me, protect me, catch me, lift me, and stretched out for me. In the name of Jesus, mighty in deed and word, I pray, amen.

WORD OF TRUTH 55

Only God can heal an unhealed heart and make a family whole again! (Ps. 147:3, KJV).

Prayer 55

Father, I pray for those who are encountering a situation for the first time. It doesn't matter what situation, whether it is medical issues, homelessness, unemployment, or the loss of a loved one. I pray that You guide them in this unchartered water. Be their friend, their light, their way, their healer, and anything they need filled. Fill them until their cup runs over. All this I pray in Jesus's name, amen.

Word of Truth 56

Your future doesn't have to be your past. Let every curse and any negative things in your family tree stop with you! (2 Cor. 5:17, KJV).

Prayer 56

Lord, I come to You on behalf of those who are divorced and raising their children on their own. Father, heal their broken hearts, build up their trust again. Let it all start with You. Touch them so that they know that You love them. Give them strength to face the day and to take care of their children. Open windows of opportunity, and do not let them lack anything. Your promises still stand—that You will heal the brokenhearted and take care of the weak. Father, I thank You, and all these things I ask, in Jesus's name, amen!

Word of Truth 57

Every healing begins with the revealing of the hurt (James 5:16, KJV).

Prayer 57

"Do nothing out of selfish ambition or vain conceit. Rather, in humility value others above yourselves, not looking to your own interests but each of you to the interests of the others. In your relationships with one another, have the same mindset as Christ Jesus" (Phil. 2:3–5, NIV). Dear Lord, please work through me and guide me so that I will have the mind of Christ in all I do. Help me that I will not do anything in the flesh and out of selfish ambition or vain conceit but that I will remain humble and never consider myself better than others. Provide the means and the desire to look after the interests of others as well as my own interests. I pray that I will have a godly attitude in all my actions and decisions and that Your love will flow through me. May I be a blessing to You and to everyone around me. In the name of Jesus I pray, amen.

Word of Truth 58

When you forgive your enemy, they may be in anguish about what they have done to you (Prov. 24:17, KJV).

Prayer 58

Dear God, thank You for all the children in the world. Everyone is precious, a heritage and gift from You. I pray for protection, guidance, good health, loving families, positive role models, and many blessings upon these children. Many are being mistreated, others are covered in love. Some are spoiled, others have nothing—not even bare necessities. Please reach out and touch them all and meet every need in the way You see well. In Jesus's name I pray, amen.

Word of Truth 59

Foolish man goes on to cursing at God, not understanding He is love. Blinded by inequity and in sin, they declare that this God is a fictitious person made up. God is a living God and still performs miracles (Jer. 10:10, KJV).

Prayer 59

Dear God of hope and promise, I pray that You will give me the patience I need to wait upon Your will and plans for me. Give me the inner peace and understanding to know Your will and the boldness to step out in faith and to do Your will. I thank You for Your promises to give wisdom, to always be there for me, to forgive me, to receive me into Your kingdom and grant eternal life through the blood and sacrifice of Jesus Christ. Thank You, my Lord, full of grace and truth. In Jesus's name, amen.

Word of Truth 60

Ladies, a man can smell your neediness a mile away. Fix yourself first! (Prov. 18:22, KJV).

Prayer 60

Dear God, here I am in awe of Your tremendous love and power. I too am persuaded that neither death nor life, neither angels nor demons, neither the present nor the future, nor any power, neither height nor depth, nor anything else in all creation, will be able to separate me from Your love that is in Christ Jesus our Lord (based on Romans 8:38–39, NIV). My identity is not in my job, my profession, nor any other thing, but in You. I am convinced that no matter what happens, I am a precious human being in Your sight, and Your love, grace, and mercy will always sustain me. Thank you so much. In Jesus's name, amen.

Word of Truth 61

God is going to bless you according to the level of your integrity (1 Kings 9:4–5, KJV).

Prayer 61

Father God, in the name of Jesus, everyone going through the valley reading this prayer will be blessed by You! For surely, O Lord, You bless the righteous. I, therefore, declare that I am blessed through Jesus Christ. Thank You for surrounding me with Your favor as with a shield. I thank You, Lord, that I can abound in Your favor and blessing today. I, therefore, expect Your favor to go before me today. I anticipate the favor of God surrounding me, and I expect my Heavenly Father to give me favor with men, even with the ungodly. In Jesus's name, amen.

Word of Truth 62

Marriage is a ministry and not sex. If you are not ready to minister, don't get into it! (Heb. 13:4, KJV).

Prayer 62

I thank You, Heavenly Father, for opening doors for me that neither man nor the devil can shut. Thank You for blessing the works of my hands as I walk under an open heaven. May I experience Your supernatural increase and provision in every area of my life this day. I choose to walk in faith and in victory. In Jesus's name I pray, amen.

WORD OF TRUTH 63

Do not get into a relationship if you are carrying junk with you, for you will drag your partner down with you. Get rid of the junk first! (Prov. 25:28, KJV).

Prayer 63

Dear God, thank You for a new day. I know that everything I am and everything I have is a result of what You have allowed in my life. Sometimes life is very hard; other times it is full of happiness. I know You are always there and Your blessing is available—if only I will listen and obey. Please help me to recognize the gifts You send and the doors You open each and every day. Give me wisdom to see and do Your will. Thank You for the spiritual gifts You have given also. I pray that You will use those gifts to work in and through me to minister to the world and draw people to You. In Jesus's name, I pray and give You praise. Amen.

WORD OF TRUTH 64

When God chooses a mate for you, they will accommodate you where you are going in life! (1 Pet 3:7, KJV).

Prayer 64

Dear precious, loving Father in heaven, thank You for Your gracious love. Thank You for the love of fellow believers. Please remind us through Your spirit that as the body of Christ, we are to encourage and exhort one another. When a brother or sister is down, we should not gossip, condemn, criticize, and "kick" them, so to speak. Instead, it is up to us to pray for, pick up the phone, or make a visit to show that we care—in love. Let us ask if they are all right and if we may pray with them. Let us be sincere in reaching out to lift them up. May we be instruments to help draw them to You, and let us not forget even one. Thank You for Your mercies. May we also be merciful. In the name of Jesus Christ, my Lord and Savior I pray, amen.

Word of Truth 65

You must have a servant heart—that is what the Lord said. Religion creates a false humility (Matt. 23:11, KJV).

Prayer 65

Dear Lord, the old hymn "Faith of Our Fathers" played in my mind today. I want to thank You that the faith of many fathers lives on. I want to thank You for the faith of those who influenced and touched my life so that I too might have faith in You. Thank You for Your word that sheds light and provides hope. Please strengthen me and grant me courage and wisdom to live such a life and take such actions that I may influence and touch other people's lives with Your great love and mercy, that they may know that You are God, the Almighty, who created us and loves us still and that they may come to know Jesus Christ as their Savior also. Please reign in my life now and forevermore. In Jesus's name I pray, amen.

WORD OF TRUTH 66

Walk in the depth of God until all the mess you were in is clear from you (Gen. 17:1, KJV).

Prayer 66

Dear God, I need to learn to take one day at a time. Your Word reminds me, "Do not worry about tomorrow, for tomorrow will worry about its own things. Sufficient for the day is its own trouble" (Matt. 6:34, ESV). I give all my worries and concerns to You, God, the all-knowing, all-powerful, and ever-present Almighty God. Please give me peace, grace, and wisdom for the day. Lord, I also pray for the people in this world who live in war-torn nations, poverty, unhappy homes, and abusive situations. Please reach down and show them Your love that they may know that You are God and that You care about them and will give them rest. In Jesus's name, amen.